Adele

young reader's library of **pop biographies**

Adele

Katy Perry

Lady Gaga

Macklemore

Nicki Minaj

young reader's library of **pop biographies**

Adele

C. F. Earl

Young Reader's Library of Pop Biographies: Adele

Copyright © 2016 by Village Earth Press, a division of Harding House Publishing. All rights reserved. No part of this publication may be reproduced or transmitted in any form or by any means, electronic or mechanical, including photocopying, recording, taping, or any information storage and retrieval system, without permission from the publisher.

Village Earth Press
Vestal, New York 13850
www.villageearthpress.com

First Printing
9 8 7 6 5 4 3 2 1

Series ISBN (paperback): 978-1-62524-441-3
ISBN (paperback): 978-1-62524-387-4
ebook ISBN: 978-1-62524-143-6
   Library of Congress Control Number: 2014933982

Author: Earl, C. F.

Table of Contents

1. On Top, Looking Back	7
2. A Star at Nineteen	17
3. Highs and Lows	27
4. Adele Today	37
Learn Even More	44
Index	46
About the Author & Picture Credits	48

Chapter One

On Top, Looking Back

Adele stood on a dark stage and began to sing for the 2012 Grammy Award Show audience. Dressed in black, she belted out the chorus to her hit "Rolling in the Deep." "We could have had it all," she sang in her powerful voice.

Just a short time before Adele's performance, many fans feared she would never sing again. She'd had to cancel a tour the year before because of a health problem that kept her from singing. The Grammy performance put fans at ease. Adele was back, shouting out one of her biggest hits. Her voice was as strong as ever.

As Adele came to the end of the chorus, a single blue light came up behind the singer. Her band began to play, and Adele continued singing with an amazing performance of the huge hit. When she ended the song, music stars like Bruno Mars and Rihanna stood and cheered for Adele.

The British singer with the stunning voice was already one of the biggest stars in the room. Her performance on the Grammy stage was just more proof of why she's become so popular. Adele's personal songs and emotional singing have earned her fans around the world.

With her second album, *21*, and songs like "Someone Like You" and "Rolling in the Deep," Adele has become one of the biggest stars in music. Her songs are on the radio. Her music videos have been watched millions and millions of times on YouTube. Adele fans are young and old, and they've bought millions of her albums.

Adele may be one of the most famous people in music today, but she wasn't always the singer fans love today. Before Adele became a music **icon**, she was a young girl growing up in north London.

EARLY LIFE

Adele's full name is Adele Laurie Blue Adkins. She was born on May 5, 1988, in Tottenham, part of London. Adele's mother is Penny Adkins, and her father was Mark Evans. When Adele was born, Penny was only eighteen years old. Mark didn't stay in his daughter's life for long. He left Penny to raise her baby Adele by herself.

> An **icon** is someone other people look up to.

Even though Mark left Penny and Adele, the mother and daughter weren't entirely alone. Adele told *Vogue Magazine* years later that her mother's family was a big part of her life as a

Music History: The Grammy Awards

The Grammys are music's most important awards. The Recording Academy founded the Grammy awards in 1959. For more than fifty years, the Grammys have given people in the music business a chance to vote on each year's best music.

In 2003, Adele's idol Etta James won the Grammy Lifetime Achievement Award. James won three Grammys during her career in music, and now Adele has already won many Grammys in her short time recording music. She's bound to win many more too. For more information about the Grammy Awards, visit www.grammy.com.

child. She said, "Even though [my mom] brought me up on her own, it was kind of a team effort."

Adele also told the magazine how much she thinks of her mother. "She's the calmest person, really strong and clever and beautiful," Adele said.

From an early age, Adele was a big fan of music. Her mother took Adele to concerts when she was just a few years old. Adele listened to all sorts of music when she was young. She also loved to sing. Adele's mother sometimes let her sing at dinner parties for her friends.

When Adele was eleven years old, Penny and Adele moved to south London. Adele made new friends who shared new R&B music with Adele. She started listening to artists like Destiny's Child and Faith Evans.

Ella Fitzgerald was one of Adele's favorite singers growing up. Adele has said voices like Ella's helped her find her own singing voice.

But her two favorite singers were from an older generation. Adele told the *Washington Post* that she found them by accident. "There was a bargain bin in the jazz section [at the store] that was, like, two CDs for like $10," she said. "I loved Etta James's big catty eyes and her blond hair. . . . I loved that [Ella Fitzgerald] was, like, you know, a big girl. As soon as I heard Ella Fitzgerald, I knew that I'd heard her voice before, but Etta James I'd never heard." She started singing along with Ella's and Etta's songs and tried to match their voices. She found her own voice by singing with them.

As a kid, Adele didn't do much more than sing for her family and with her friends. But soon, she'd do much more with her strong voice and love for music.

SINGING IN SCHOOL

When she was fourteen years old, Adele started going to a new school, the BRIT School for Performing Arts and Technology. The London school teaches many young people about music, visual art, dance, and other arts. For Adele, the BRIT school was the place she could begin to chase her dreams.

At first, though, Adele told the website BluesandSoul.com, she didn't want to go to the BRIT school. But soon, that all changed. Adele said that the school "had free rehearsal rooms with free equipment, where I was listening to music all day for years."

She added, "[It] was really **inspiring** to wake up every day to go to school with kids that actually

> Something or someone **inspiring** pushes others to do great things.

The BRIT School

The BRIT School has become famous for helping young artists become the stars of tomorrow. The British Government and the British Record Industry Trust started the school in the early 1990s. Today, the BRIT School teaches students from fourteen to nineteen years old about the arts. The school has classes for students interested in music, film, photography, painting, and more.

wanted to be **productive** at something and wanted to be somebody."

Adele told the *Guardian* that she learned a lot at the BRIT School. She learned how to record music in a studio. She learned about the business of music. By the time she left the BRIT School, Adele was ready to find her place in the music world. But even after learning so much, she would still have to work hard to reach her dreams.

STARTING IN MUSIC

Adele began writing songs while she was a teenager. A friend helped her put recordings of Adele's songs on the Internet. Starting in 2004, Adele used MySpace to share her music with people online.

In 2006, Adele graduated from the BRIT School, ready to start working to become a professional singer. In the same year,

Music History: XL Recordings

XL has worked with a huge number of artists from the United States and the UK. The record label has released music from the White Stripes, Vampire Weekend, and M.I.A., as well as many others. The label started putting out music in 1989, at first just releasing music by a few little-known artists. By the early 2000s, however, the small record company had become a successful business. The company is best known for taking risks on new artists and helping them to become popular.

Nick Huggett found Adele's music on MySpace and wanted to help her start her music career. Nick worked at XL Recordings, a record company that works with artists to sell music. Soon, Adele had a deal with XL to record and sell her music. She would have the chance to record an album and get more people to listen to her voice.

Adele was on her way to her dream. Soon, she would find more success in music than many people do in a lifetime.

> Being **productive** means working hard to get things done.

On Top, Looking Back

Find Out Even More

Reading books is one of the best ways to find out about the music and artists you love. One book can't hold all of the facts you want to know about your favorite stars or musical styles, though. Each author has to choose what to include. Some facts or stories they choose to put in the book. Others they have to leave out. Always remember that to get a bigger picture, you have to read more than one book.

Your school or local library is the first place to look for books about the subjects you find interesting. Start by checking the library's card catalog. Many libraries have electronic catalogs you can search through, too. If you can't find what you're looking for, ask a librarian for help. See if you can find any of the books listed below. If you can't find these books, try looking for other books about music, singers, or soul music.

Anniss, Matt. *The Story of Soul and R&B (Pop Histories)*. North Mankato, Minn.: Smart Apple Media, 2013.

Handyside, Christopher. *Soul and R&B (History of American Music)*. North Mankato, Minn.: Heinemann-Raintree, 2005.

Krohn, Katherine E. *Ella Fitzgerald: First Lady of Song (Carter G. Woodson Honor Book)*. Minneapolis, Minn.: Lerner Publishing Group, 2001.

Once you've found a few books, take a look at the table of contents. Look over the names of the chapters and flip to a chapter that sounds interesting to you. Ask yourself a few questions as you read the chapter you picked:

1. How is the book organized? Can you easily find information that you're looking for? Use the table of contents and index together to find the facts you want to read about
2. Does the book have pictures? How do the pictures help you understand what the book is about?
3. Do you have a hard time reading the book or understanding the text? Each book is written for a different audience, and not every book is meant for every reader. Finding a book that you can read and understand is important to becoming a better reader. Challenging yourself is important as well, but reading a book you can't understand won't help you learn about your favorite music.
4. What do you think of the book? Do you like it? Would you read more? Why or why not?

Chapter Two

A Star at Nineteen

Adele had a record deal with XL Recordings, but now she had to make an album. Having a big company behind her would help get her music into stores, but she had to write and record songs first. Adele had been writing songs for a while now—but soon, the whole world would hear the songs Adele wrote in her bedroom.

ADELE'S FIRST ALBUM

One of the songs Adele wrote when she was still in school, when she was only sixteen, was called "Hometown Glory." Adele has said the song is the first she ever wrote. At the end of 2007, Adele released a new recording of the song that would also be on her first album. It came out as the first single for her album in the UK. The song became popular in Adele's home country and helped her to gain some early success before she put out her album.

Adele released her first album, *19*, in early 2008. The album came out in January in the UK and February in the United States. In its first week out, *19* earned the number-one position on the UK album charts, selling more than any other album that week. In its first week of release in the United States, though, Adele's album came in lower on the *Billboard* charts than it did in Adele's home country.

Adele chose her album's name because she was nineteen years old when she worked on many of the songs for the album. Adele wanted her album to show who she was at the time she was making it. The title was a part of that. The album's songs were the rest.

Adele talked to the website BluesandSoul.com about the title of the album. "I was only nineteen years old when I was writing it, and I just kinda remember becoming a bit of a woman during that time," she said. "And I think that is definitely **documented** in the songs."

Adele's released a single from her album called "Chasing Pavements." The song was released before the album and soon became a hit in the UK and the United States. In the United States, the song reached number 21 on the *Billboard* Hot 100 songs chart. The music video played on television and fans watched it online. The success of "Chasing Pavements" earned Adele many new fans around the world.

Adele also put out other singles from *19*. After the success of "Chasing Pavements,"

> Something that has been **documented** has been written down or recorded.

Music History: The *Billboard* Charts

Started in 1894, *Billboard* magazine first showed readers where they could find exciting entertainment. Years later, the magazine began to focus on music. In the 1930s and '40s, *Billboard* started recording which music was most popular with listeners. *Billboard* created different charts to keep track of the popularity of different kinds of music. Over time, the music business began to see the *Billboard* charts as the ultimate sign of success. Artists hope to get a number-one song or album.

Adele made *Billboard*-chart history in 2011. She became the first woman to earn the number-one spot on *Billboard's* end-of-year artist, album, and pop song charts. Her song "Rolling in the Deep" was bigger than any other pop song during 2011, according to *Billboard's* charts.

she released "Cold Shoulder" and "Make You Feel My Love." The songs didn't become quite as popular as the album's first hit single, but they were successful.

Adele also went on television to help spread the word about her album. She appeared on shows in the United States and the UK. She performed on shows like *Saturday Night Live* and *The Ellen DeGeneres Show*, gaining new fans with each song.

Adele's album *19* was a success. In the space of a few months, Adele had gone from learning about being a professional musician at school to being a famous artist. Soon, she'd be winning Grammys and going on world tours.

Adele won both Grammy Awards she was nominated for in 2009, giving her a place as a young star in the music world.

ADELE'S FIRST GRAMMYS

At the 2009 Grammy Awards, Adele was **nominated** for two Grammys. She was nominated for Best New Artist, and her song "Chasing Pavements" was nominated for Best Female Pop Vocal Performance.

On the night of the awards show, Adele also performed "Chasing Pavements" with country singer Jennifer Nettles. Adele's performance, followed by her two big Grammy wins, was a big accomplishment for the young singer.

Adele would win more Grammys, but winning her first Grammys were important. She was excited as she took the stage to accept the Best New Artist award.

"Thank you so much," Adele told the crowd. "I'm going to cry!"

Adele went on to thank the people who had helped her reach success, including her mother and XL Recordings. Before she left the stage, Adele didn't forget the other artists nominated for Best New Artist.

"Duffy, I love you, I think you're amazing. Jonas Brothers, I love you as well," Adele said before walking off the stage in tears.

> When someone is **nominated**, she is chosen to be part of a group competing for an award.

Adele's first Grammy Awards show was a big night for the singer. Many people who had never heard of Adele got to hear her sing at the Grammy Awards show for the first time. With

A Star at Nineteen

During her first tour, Adele performed at the famous Hollywood Bowl outdoor arena in Los Angeles, California.

millions of people watching, Adele had a great opportunity to show off her amazing voice. After Adele's big Grammy wins, thousands of people bought her album, *19*. The album even reached the top ten on *Billboard* after Adele's big night.

AN EVENING WITH ADELE

After Adele put out her first album, she started a tour to perform for her fans. Adele called her tour "An Evening with Adele." Adele performed in Europe and North America during the tour. With the success of *19*, new fans were excited to see Adele in concert.

Adele toured the world for more than a year. She began her tour in Europe in January of 2008, singing for fans in England, Ireland, and Germany. Then she crossed the Atlantic to perform for North American fans in New York, Toronto, and Los Angeles.

Adele's first big tour was a success. By the time Adele finished her tour in the summer of 2009, she'd performed dozens of times for thousands of fans.

With Adele's album *19*, her tour, and her two wins at the Grammy Awards, the British singer had already become famous. She had gained fans and sold hundreds of thousands of albums. Adele won awards and performed on television in Britain and the United States.

Soon, she would have even more success. Millions of people around the world would be listening to her now. The album *19* had been a hit—but her next album would do even better.

Find Out Even More

Books aren't the only place you can learn more about music and the musicians you love. On the Internet, you can find all the information you want to know about almost any topic. When you use the Internet, however, you have to find all the information yourself. A book's author picks the information for you. She puts the facts and stories together in a way that gives you a certain view of a subject. Online, you'll have to find the facts and stories you want to know using search engines like Google, Bing, or Yahoo. Then you'll have to put the information together in your mind and make sense of it for yourself.

Search engines help you sort through all of the information on different websites on the Internet. Websites like Google.com are made to help people find new information by typing in a few keywords. Typing a few words into the Google search bar can take you to millions of websites about the subject that interests you. Be careful when picking your keywords, though. The wrong keywords won't get you the information about Adele's career or the history of soul music you want to find.

Here are some keywords to use online to find out more about Adele's story. Which ones get you the most information?

Tottenham
The Grammys
Ella Fitzgerald
Etta James
"Rolling in the Deep"
history of soul music
R&B music
The BRIT School

Chapter Three

Highs and Lows

Adele took some time off after her tour, and then she began working on her second album. During her time away, she had gone through a rough breakup with a boyfriend—so when Adele came to putting new songs together, she had heartbreak on her mind.

Adele's album *21* would soon become one of the most successful albums in recent years. The album would make Adele an even bigger star and win her millions of new fans. But its songs were inspired by a tough time in Adele's life. Getting over an old boyfriend can be hard for anyone. Luckily, Adele could sing about the pain and anger that she felt. And soon, fans around the world would be singing along with every word.

MORE SUCCESS WITH *21*

Adele put out her second album, *21*, in early 2011, almost exactly three years after she had released her first. Adele said she wasn't sure about naming the album *21* at first. She told

Lead singer from the band One Republic, Ryan Tedder (center), helped Adele write "Turning Tables" and "Rumour Has It" for Adele's *21*.

Interview Magazine that at first she didn't want to name her second album after her age as she did with her first. But then she saw things differently.

"I'd be like, 'No, I'll have an imagination thank you very much, I'm not going to carry it on,'" she said. "And then when it came to naming this record it was the only relevant thing, because my relationship that the entire record is about was about me coming of age. And 21 is the age when you're suddenly a proper adult and on your own."

In some ways, Adele's fans can watch her grow up by listening to each of her albums. Each tells a story about what Adele's life is like at the time she made it. And Adele's fans were ready to hear more from the singer.

Adele created many of the songs on her second album with a man named Paul Epworth. Paul had worked in music for years, helping bands and artists find their voices. He and Adele worked closely together on *21*. The two made some of Adele's biggest songs from her second album. Adele would work with Paul for years to come, as well.

During the recording of her second album, Adele also worked with Ryan Tedder, singer from the band One Republic. A famous music producer named Rick Rubin worked on *21* with Adele too. Rick has worked with **legendary** artists like the Beastie Boys, Jay-Z, Johnny Cash, and Lady Gaga. He recorded a few songs for *21* with Adele.

In its first week out, *21* quickly became a

> Someone **legendary** is very famous and well-known for a long time.

Highs and Lows 29

The Royal Albert Hall in London has been host to some of the most amazing artists in musical history, including Adele.

Music History: Royal Albert Hall

Royal Albert Hall is one of the most famous places in musical history. Since it was opened in 1871, the most talented musicians have performed at Royal Albert Hall. From classical pianist and composer Sergei Rachmaninov to rock band Led Zeppelin, Albert Hall has been home to amazing musical performances for more than a century. In recent years, artists like rapper Jay-Z, rock band the Killers, and Adele herself have kept alive the tradition of amazing concerts at Royal Albert Hall. For more information about Royal Albert Hall, visit www.royalablerthall.com

huge success. As she had done with her first album, Adele put out the album first in the UK and then a month later in the United States. In its first week of release in the UK, the album sold more than 200,000 copies, more than any other album sold that week. In the United States, the album took the top spot on the Billboard album charts in its first week out. In just one week, 21 sold more than 350,000 copies in the United States.

The album had a group of smash singles. Adele's first single from her new album was "Rolling in the Deep." The song, written by Adele and Paul, was also the first on the album. "Rolling in the Deep" was a hit in the UK as soon as Adele released the song near the end of 2010. In the United States, the song's success took some time to grow. Eventually, the song would make it to number one on the *Billboard* Hot 100 songs chart.

Adele's next single was "Someone Like You," the last song on *21*. Like "Rolling in the Deep," the song was a big hit in the

UK right away. Over time, the song became a number-one hit in the United States, as well, after Adele had performed the song for new audiences.

Many artists hope for just one number-one song on the *Billboard* charts. With *21*, Adele had three. The third single "Set Fire to the Rain" also reached the top of the Hot 100 chart. Other singles "Rumour Has It" and "Turning Tables" were also big hits around the world, though they didn't do quite as well as Adele's other singles on the U.S. charts.

Adele's *21* was number one on the *Billboard* album charts for months. The album broke the record for the longest time in the top spot on the album chart in its twenty-first week at number one. The album sold millions and millions of copies to fans around the world. The strong singing and touching songwriting on *21* had made Adele an even bigger star.

After releasing *21*, Adele began to tour the world again. During 2011, she performed around the world on her "Adele Live" tour.

While on tour, Adele performed at the historic Royal Albert Hall in London. She recorded the performance for a live DVD that she released later in the year called *Live at the Royal Albert Hall*. Fans who didn't get to see Adele on tour now had a chance to see the singer in concert at one of the most famous places a musician can perform.

ADELE LOSES HER VOICE

While on tour, Adele woke up one morning and made a Skype call. She found she couldn't speak at all. Her voice was completely gone.

For a singer like Adele, losing your voice is very scary. Singing isn't just Adele's passion; it's also her job. She worried something was wrong, but she told herself things would be fine. Soon, however, she had to cancel shows because she couldn't sing. In October 2011, Adele wrote to her fans on her website about the problems she was having with her voice.

"I first started having trouble with my voice back in January," Adele wrote. "It was weakened by a bout of flu from December and never got its complete strength back before I started my UK and European . . . tour, so it just got weaker and weaker until it eventually 'broke.'"

Adele promised she would try to take good care of her voice. She wrote to her fans that she was listening to doctors who told her how to care for her voice and following their instructions. But her singing problems continued during her 2011 tour. Adele told her fans she was "heartbroken" that she would have to cancel her tour so that she could rest her voice.

Adele had to have surgery on her vocal cords to repair the damage that had been done to them. Adele had what is called a vocal hemorrhage. Doctors told Adele that the injury is a bit like a black eye on the vocal cords. The bruising on Adele's vocal cords would need to heal. She stayed away from singing altogether for a little while. After that, she had to start working to build the strength in her voice again.

Fans worried that one of their favorite singers was finished making music. But Adele wouldn't keep her fans waiting for long. Soon, her vocal cords would be better—and she would be singing for her millions of fans again.

Find Out Even More

Try searching for Adele on Google.com and you'll find millions of results. Here are some of the results from the first page for her name:

ADELE
www.adele.tv
Adele - Wikipedia, the free encyclopedia
en.wikipedia.org/wiki/Adele
Adele - Rolling in the Deep - YouTube
www.youtube.com/watch?v=rYEDA3JcQqw
Adele - Someone Like You - YouTube
www.youtube.com/watch?v=hLQl3WQQoQ0
Adele | New Music And Songs | MTV
www.mtv.com/artists/adele
Adele (OfficialAdele) on Twitter
twitter.com/OfficialAdele

Not every site you find when using a search engine like Google will get you just what you want to find. Which of the sites above is the best source of information about Adele's music and life?

Adele.tv is Adele's official site. The official site of any artist is usually the best place to find information about new music and important announcements. Adele and many other artists also use social media to speak to their fans online. Adele's official Twitter and Facebook page are good places to find new information about the British singer. On Twitter, look for a "verified" checkmark, so you can be sure that you're hearing from the artist herself. Sometimes, social media is more about opinion than fact, so make sure you know who is posting to these sites when you're looking for news about your favorite artists.

    Fan websites can be another good source of information about music and singers. Fan sites are run by people who truly care about the artist and want to get good information to other fans. But the artists don't run fan websites. Always remember that a fan page isn't official. Fans may post something that isn't true. Official sources of information about artists are usually a better place to find facts.

    Wikipedia can be a good place to start looking for information online about a topic you find interesting. But don't take everything you read on Wikipedia as true without checking the facts. Facts posted to Wikipedia should have small numbers next to them you can click on to visit the website that is the source of the information. Checking the facts and sources is the best way to be sure you are reading true information about the music and artists you love.

Chapter Four

Adele Today

After Adele lost her voice, many fans were worried she would have trouble singing in the future. But soon, news came that she'd be taking the stage again in February 2012. Adele told fans that she would be performing at the 2012 Grammy Awards Show.

ADELE'S BIG NIGHT

Adele told the BBC she was nervous after losing her voice but excited to be part of one of the biggest nights in music.

"It's an absolute honor to be included in such a night," Adele said. "And for it to be my first performance in months is very exciting and of course nerve-racking but what a way to get back into it all."

By the night of the Grammys, Adele was ready. She blew away the audience with her song "Rolling in the Deep."

Adele's amazing performance wasn't the only highlight of the night for the British singer. She was also nominated for six

Grammys in 2012. Her album *21* was nominated for Best Pop Vocal Album and Album of the Year. "Rolling in the Deep" was nominated for Song of the Year, Record of the Year, and Best Music Video. Adele was also nominated for Best Pop Solo Performance for "Someone Like You."

Out of all the Grammys for which Adele had been nominated, she ended up winning every single one, taking home all six. It's rare for an artist to take home more than one Grammy in a single night, but winning six is incredible!

After her big night at the Grammy Awards, fans knew Adele was back. But no one was sure what was next for the British singer. Adele wouldn't keep her fans waiting long for another big song.

A SONG FOR *SKYFALL*

At the end of 2011, Adele had told fans that she would be working on a special song. She would be recording a song for the 2012 James Bond movie, *Skyfall*. Many famous singers and musicians have recorded songs for the James Bond movies. Now Adele would earn another spot in music history by recording a song for the hit series.

Adele said that at first she wasn't sure if she wanted to do a song for *Skyfall*. "There's a lot of instant spotlight and pressure when it comes to a Bond song," she told the official James Bond website (www.007.com). "But I fell in love with the **script** and Paul [Epworth] had some great ideas for the track and it ended up being a bit of a no brainer to do it in the end."

A **script** is the written text actors speak during a movie, play, or TV show.

Music History: The Songs of James Bond

Each time James Bond saves the world on the big screen, his movies have a big song from a famous artist. Since 1962, James Bond has been the main character in more than twenty movies. The Bond movies have had songs from artists like Tina Turner, Paul McCartney, Madonna, and Alicia Keys. Songs from James Bond movies have gone on to win Oscars and become part of music history. Adele is the latest artist to create new music for a James Bond movie. But she certainly won't be the last. Bond is bound to beat the bad guys in movies for years to come.

Adele released her new song, "Skyfall," on October 5th, 2012, almost exactly a year after she told fans she had lost her voice. October 5th was also the fiftieth anniversary of the opening day of the first James Bond movie, *Dr. No*.

Not long after its release, Adele's song became a big hit. "Skyfall" played on the radio, and the video played on television. Fans loved the first new Adele song since her album *21*. With another hit song, Adele was headed for even more success.

In 2013, Adele won two Grammys for "Skyfall." With her wins at the 2013 Grammy Awards, Adele had won eleven Grammys since she released her first album. Many musicians and singers work their entire lives without winning a single Grammy, let alone more than ten in less than five years!

Adele arrives at the 2013 Oscar Award Show. Later in the night, Adele would win for her song "Skyfall."

Adele also performed at the Oscar Awards in February. The Oscars are the most important awards in movies. Each year, the Oscars give an award to the best song recorded for a movie. In 2013, Adele's song "Skyfall" was nominated for Best Original Song. At the 85th Academy Awards show, Adele didn't just perform her hit. She also walked away an Oscar winner.

LOOKING TO THE FUTURE

With the success of her first two albums and her song for *Skyfall*, Adele has become one of the world's biggest music stars. She has millions of fans around the world singing along with her songs. Today, fans wait eagerly for new music from Adele. They check music websites and Twitter for any news about the British singer's next move.

Adele's songs are personal. Things happening in her own life inspire her to write songs. Whatever happens next for Adele, her fans are sure to hear about it—good or bad—on her next album. And they couldn't be more excited to share in her joy and her pain.

Find Out Even More

No two websites are exactly alike. Each website is made for a different reason. Some people make websites to give people facts, and others want to share their opinions online. Other websites are trying to sell something. Knowing who made the website and why they wanted to make it is a big part of judging websites. To find the information that best matches what you're looking for online, it's a good idea to ask yourself a few questions as you're browsing each website you visit:

1. Who made the website? Try to find an "About Us" page on the website to help you figure out who made the site and why. What does the site tell you about why it was made? What is the site meant to give to people who visit it? Knowing who made the website and what its goal is helps you find better information on the Internet. Not every website is a good source of information. Some sites won't do much to help you find the information you need.
2. When was the website made? How long has it been since the website was updated? If no one has updated the website for a while, chances are good things have changed since the information was posted. You'll want to find newer information on another website.

3. Is the website easy to use? Is there a search bar that can help you find what you're looking for? How quickly can you find what you're looking for on the website?
4. Is the information you're reading on this website available on other websites? Is this website the source of the information or is the information from another source? Can you find the source of the information?
5. Can you find the information in a book? Can you find books that support the information on the website? Often, using books and the Internet together is the best way to find the facts about a topic that interests you.

Learn Even More

IN BOOKS

Azzarelli, Ally. *Adele! Singing Sensation (Sizzling Celebrities)*. Berkeley Heights, N.J.: Enslow Publishing, Inc., 2013.

Gagne, Tammy. *Adele (Blue Banner Biographies)*. Hockessin, Del.: Mitchell Lane Publishers, 2012.

McDowell, Pamela. *Adele (Remarkable People)*. New York: AV2 By Weigl, 2013.

Tieck, Sarah. *Adele: Singing Sensation (Big Buddy Biographies)*. Minneapolis, Minn.: Big Buddy Books, 2013.

ONLINE

Adele on AllMusic
www.allmusic.com/artist/adele-mn0000503460

Adele on Billboard.com
www.billboard.com/artist/278035/adele

Adele's Official Website
www.adele.tv

Adele's Official Twitter Account
twitter.com/OfficialAdele

Adele's Record Company, XL Recordings
www.xlrecordings.com/adele

Index

19 (album) 18–19, 23
21 (album) 8, 18, 27–29, 31–32, 38–39

"Adele Live" (tour) 32
Adkins, Penny 8
"An Evening with Adele" (tour) 23

BBC 37
Billboard charts 18–19, 32
Bond, James 38–39
BRIT School, the 11–12, 25

"Chasing Pavements" 18, 21

Evans, Mark 8–9

fans 7–9, 18–19, 23, 27, 29, 32–33, 35, 37–39, 41
father 8
Fitzgerald, Ella 10–11, 15, 25

Grammy Awards, the 9, 20–21, 23, 37–39
Guardian 12

Huggett, Nick 13

Interview Magazine 29

James, Etta 9, 11, 25, 38–39

Live at the Royal Albert Hall 32
London 8–9, 11, 30, 32

mother 8–9, 21
MySpace 12

Oscars 39, 41

R&B 9, 14, 25
"Rolling in the Deep" 7–8, 19, 25, 31, 37–38
Royal Albert Hall 30–32

Rubin, Rick 29
"Rumour Has It" 28, 32

"Set Fire to the Rain" 32
Skyfall 38–41
"Someone Like You" 8, 31, 34, 38
soul 14, 24–25

Tedder, Ryan 28–29

Tottenham 8, 25
"Turning Tables" 28, 32

Vogue Magazine 8

Washington Post 11

XL Recordings 13, 17, 21, 45

About the Author

C.F. Earl is a writer living and working in Binghamton, New York. Earl writes on a range of topics, including pop culture, history, and health.

Picture Credits

Dreamstime.com:
    Carrienelson1: p. 26, 28
    Dmitry Naumov: p. 30
    Featureflash: p. 40

Sbukley: pp. 6, 16, 20, 36

Matthew Field: p. 22

www.ingramcontent.com/pod-product-compliance
Lightning Source LLC
Chambersburg PA
CBHW041307110426
42743CB00037B/27